This book belongs to

Name

_____

All kids are created different.

Some kids are fast.

Zoom

Some walk slow

Some would rather not be fast or slow.

I don't want to race.

Some kids are tall.

Some kids are short

and may need a little help sometimes reaching things.

And some haven't reached their height at all.

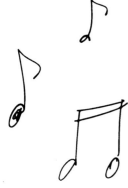

Some kids like music.

Some kids like to read.

Some like to draw.

All kids are different
and there's only one you!

Don't try and be the same as all the other kids, to fit in.
You weren't created to fit in.

You weren't created to fit in.

Color the world with your unique light.

You are very special and one of a kind.

Be the greatest you, YOU can be!

Remember to be you,
shine your light, in whatever you do.

You have a special gift of being you.

If you like to dance.
Dance your special way.

Ice cream?
What is YOUR favorite flavor?

If you like to sing,
sing your special way.

Share what you
like with others.

You have your gifts, to share.

Reading to someone can be fun!

Short or tall doesn't matter at all, **when you have a friend.**

If you like to draw you can draw a nice picture for a friend or family member. This is spreading your kindness through your light.

Only YOU can create.

HAPPY

How can you share your light with someone?

 Three ways I can shine my individual light for others to see.

1 _____

2 _____

3 _____

You can start by shining your light at home.
Maybe, help your mom with dishes.

Help pick up your toys.
This can be an act of kindness.

BE KIND
BE BRAVE
BE SILLY
BE HONEST
BE HAPPY
BE YOU

ALWAYS CHOOSE KINDNESS

You have the super power
of being you!

Just be YOU!

By; Sonya M. Davis

ISBN: 9798396991163
Imprint: Independently Published

Made in the USA
Coppell, TX
15 September 2023

21608920R00021